Weather

Contents

 Look and put the sticker.

windy

cold

cloudy

sunny

 Put sticker on the word.

How's the weather?

It's [sunny] .

 Ask and say.

Color and say.

cloudy

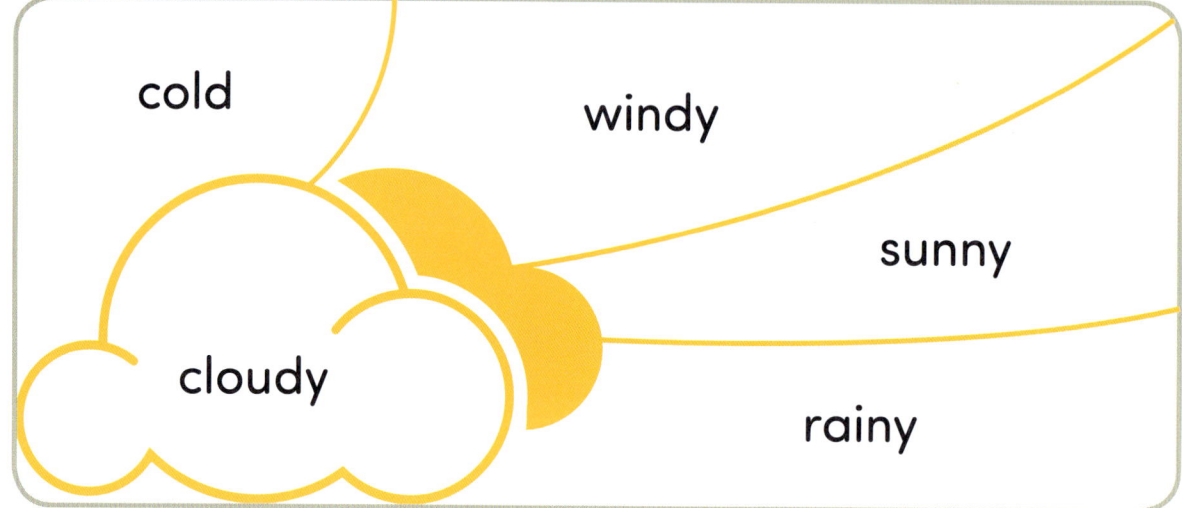

cold

windy

sunny

cloudy

rainy

cold

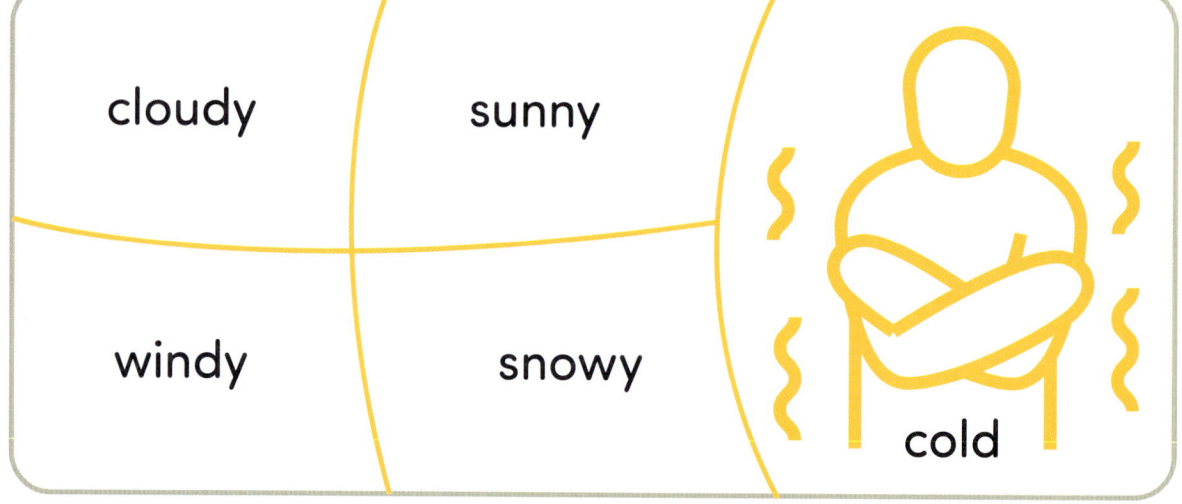

cloudy

sunny

windy

snowy

cold

 Look and put the sticker.

rainy

foggy

hot

snowy

 **Put sticker on the word.**

How's the weather?

It's rainy .

 Ask and say.

p. 2

 p. 3

sunny

 p. 5

 p. 6

rainy

 Sticker

 Good work!

 Wonderful work!

 Great effort!

 For working hard!

 Good work!

 Excellent!

 Well done!

 Well done!

 Special award!

Color.

sunny

windy

Sticker

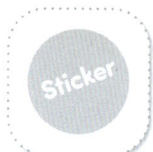

Put weather stickers and kid stickers.

rainy	sunny
snowy	windy

foggy

cloudy

hot

cold